AF075516

THE STORY BEHIND SKYDIVING

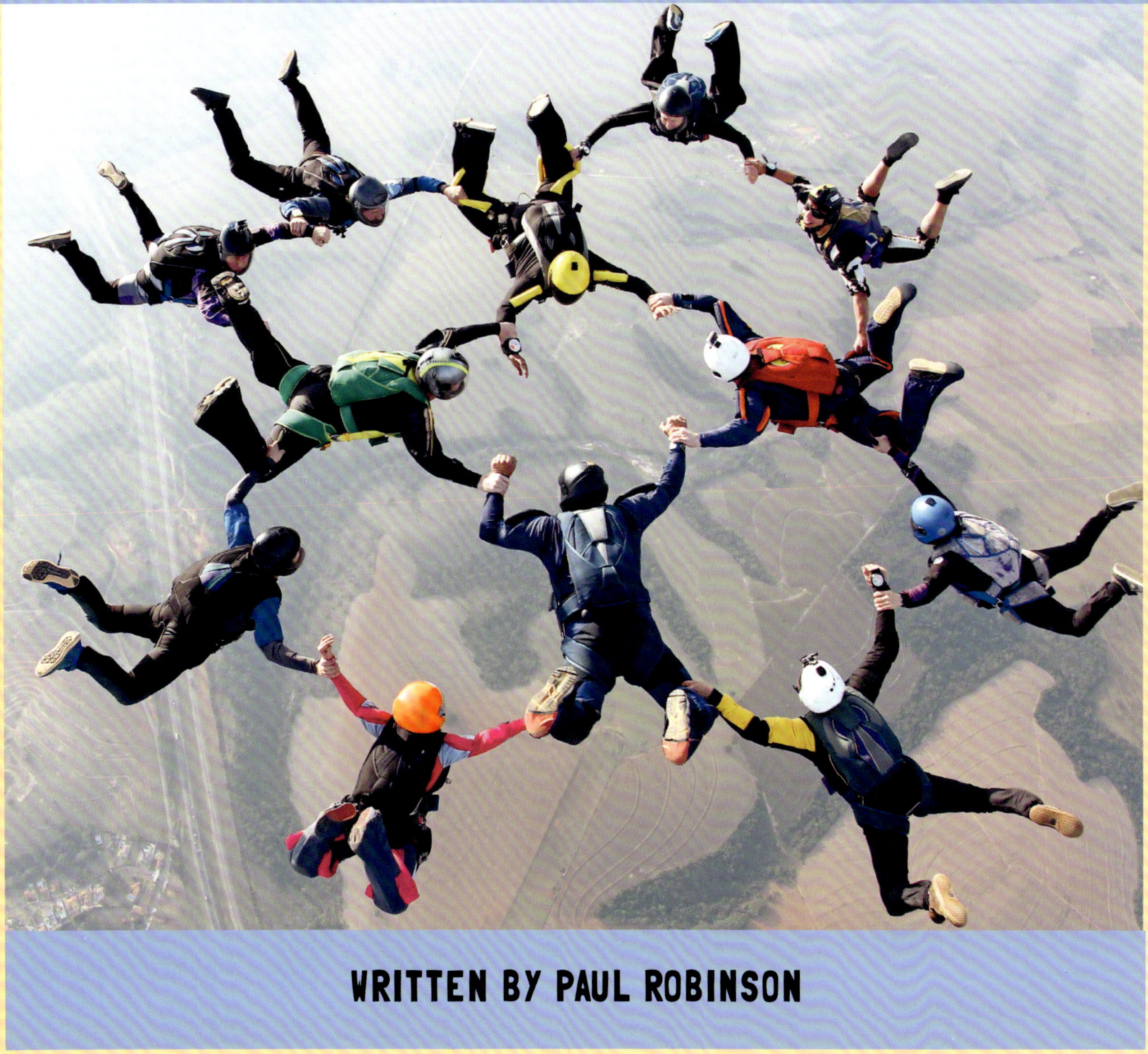

WRITTEN BY PAUL ROBINSON

CONTENTS

INTRODUCTION TO SKYDIVING	4	ON THE LINE	12
SKYDIVING GEAR	6	OUT ON YOUR OWN	14
SKYDIVING EQUIPMENT	8	DOWN TO EARTH	16
IT TAKES TWO	10	TEAM SKYDIVING	18

DISCLAIMER:

The activities in this book have been performed by people who are experienced professionals, or by people who have had professional training. Neither the publisher nor the author shall be liable for any bodily harm or damage to property whatsoever that may be caused or sustained as a result of conducting any of the activities featured in this book.

Words in **BOLD** can be found in the glossary.

OUT THERE	20	RECORD BREAKERS	28
SKY HIGH	22	GLOSSARY	30
DARING BASE JUMPING	24	INDEX	31
WORLD-CLASS SKYDIVING	26		

INTRODUCTION TO SKYDIVING

Skydiving is parachuting with a plus. The skydiver jumps from an **aircraft** and falls for about 45 seconds before opening the parachute. The time in the air before the parachute opens is called freefall.

FALLING WITH STYLE

Most skydivers use rectangular parachutes, which are easier to control than circular ones. They usually jump from aircraft flying at about 3 kilometres (10,000 ft) in the air and can hit speeds of 120 miles per hour (195 km/h) in freefall.

As the ground gets closer, they have to decide exactly when to open the parachute. Enjoying the jump safely is what this sport is all about!

DID YOU KNOW?

Parachutes were invented almost 250 years ago, but the sport of skydiving only developed about 50 years ago. Now, there are around 3.7 million jumps a year, all over the world!

TYPES OF SKYDIVING

There are many different types of skydiving!

FREEFALL

TANDEM

SOLO

FORMATION

STATIC LINE JUMP

WINGSUIT

SKYDIVING GEAR

There's no doubt that skydiving is a thrilling sport, but safety is the top priority. The right gear must be worn on every jump; this helps protect skydivers from the conditions of the fall, and in case anything goes wrong.

PARACHUTES
Skydivers always wear a main parachute, and a **reserve parachute** in case things go wrong. These are kept in a skydive backpack.

JUMPSUIT
A jumpsuit helps skydivers move through the air, and helps keep them warm when falling.

HELMET
A helmet must always be worn. This protects the head in a collision or hard landing.

GOGGLES
All skydivers need to protect their eyes. Some wear goggles, while others wear a helmet with a visor.

ALTIMETER
Altimeters show skydivers how far they are from the ground. They look like big watches and are usually worn on the wrist or hand.

SKYDIVING EQUIPMENT

It's not just wearing all the correct gear that helps to keep skydivers safe during their daring jumps. Learning how to use the equipment correctly is an essential part of skydive training.

TOGGLES
These are the brakes of the parachute. Toggles can also be used to steer.

BREAK LINES
These connect the back of the **canopy** to the toggles.

HARNESS
The harness keeps the parachutes and the skydiver attached to each other!

Some safety devices are built into the skydiving **rig** or are so small that you can't really see them!

One of the most important things is the automatic activation device (AAD) which automatically releases the main parachute when you reach a certain **altitude**. It also releases the reserve parachute if the main one fails.

Some companies now make GPS-tracking devices that alert skydivers to changes in speed so they can adjust their flight and stay safe.

DID YOU KNOW?

Experienced skydivers often carry a knife so that they can cut through lines if they get tangled.

TRUE STORY

US Army Captain Albert Berry made the first parachute jump from a moving plane over Missouri, USA, in 1912.

IT TAKES TWO

For most people, their first jump is a tandem jump with an instructor. A special harness attaches the student to the instructor, who carries the parachute. Tandem jumps are good for beginners because the instructor decides when to open the parachute.

FLYING HIGH

For a tandem jump, the plane goes up to around 3 kilometres (10,000 ft). Freefall only lasts about 45 seconds, but the instructor and student reach speeds of up to 120 mph (195 km/h). When they reach 1,500 metres (5,000 ft) above the ground, the instructor pulls the ripcord, pulling the pilot parachute out of the backpack, and opening the main parachute.

SLOWING THE DIVE

Tandem divers need larger parachutes than solo skydivers as the extra weight makes them fall quicker! They release a drogue when they jump from the plane – this is a mini-parachute which slows their fall.

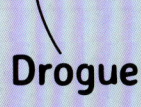

Drogue

In a tandem flight, the student is in front of the instructor.

DID YOU KNOW?

If a parachute is looked after properly, it may be used hundreds, or even thousands, of times.

ON THE LINE

Static line jumps give skydivers a taste of going solo. There is no instructor, but students do get help. A line links their parachute to a strong point inside the plane. When they jump, the line from the plane pulls the parachute open.

GOING SOLO

During a static line jump, the skydiver will fall for between 3-5 seconds before the parachute opens. This is probably the scariest part! Once the parachute is open, it will take the skydiver about three minutes to reach the ground.

SAFETY FIRST

Students need around six hours of training before their first static line jump. They learn how to exit the plane safely, guide their parachute, and land safely.

DID YOU KNOW?

Students making a first-time static line jump are usually in radio contact with instructors on the ground (through their helmets), who talk to them as they complete their dive.

OUT ON YOUR OWN

Skydivers want to go solo as soon as possible. But they must train hard for their first solo jump. There are many important things to learn before it's safe to skydive on your own.

MOVING ON

Students usually learn to skydive through an official training course such as Accelerated Freefall (AFF). On an AFF course, students have to pass each level of training before moving onto the next. Earning the right to go solo takes most students 18 practice jumps.

LICENSE TO JUMP

As well as practical training, students must pass a written exam. If they pass all of this, they can call themselves a licensed skydiver!

DID YOU KNOW?
Every jump is different, even for experienced divers!

TRUE STORY

In Canada in 1994, skydiver Sharon McClelland fell 3 kilometres (10,000 ft) when her parachutes failed to open fully. Luckily, she landed in a muddy marsh and was unharmed. Not all people are so lucky.

DOWN TO EARTH

Skydivers aim for drop zones – areas kept clear for landings – which are marked so they can be seen from the air. Skydivers steer their parachutes by pulling on the cords that attach it to the harness.

EASY DOES IT

The drop zone is a large, open area of a field or airfield kept clear of aircraft for safety. Skydivers must steer away from any other skydivers coming in to land at the same time. The slower they are going, the easier this is.

ON THE SPOT

Experienced skydivers become incredible at steering parachutes. There are world championships for accuracy landings, where skydivers compete to land the closest to a tiny disc that's just 2 cm (0.8 inches) wide – that's smaller than a coin!

DID YOU KNOW?

Skydivers heading for the drop zone slow their decent by pulling on both steering toggles at the same time. This is known as flaring, and it slows the parachute enough for a soft landing.

TEAM SKYDIVING

Jumping as part of a skydiving team takes things to a new level! If one person loses control, the whole team will be in danger. The best team skydivers react quickly to what others are doing. When things go right, they are incredible!

FORMATION SKYDIVING

These teams show off their skills in freefall. They work together to make shapes, like circles and diamonds, and other patterns in the sky. Teams can be made of any number, from 2 people to 20 plus! In competitions, most teams are made of 4 or 8 people, plus a videographer.

CANOPY FORMATION

Canopy stacking teams make shapes in the air by steering together and linking their parachutes once they've been opened. They must be careful to make sure they don't get tangled.

SHOWING OFF THEIR SKILLS

Display teams are often hired to perform at events like fairs, carnivals, and sport matches. Sometimes skydivers perform by leaving trails of smoke behind as they speed through the air.

DID YOU KNOW?

The biggest formation skydive ever was made up of 400 skydivers! It happened in Thailand in 2006 and the formation lasted 4.3 seconds. This world record is yet to be beaten.

TRUE STORY

There is an American display team called "The Flying Elvi". The members dress up as Elvis Presley for their skydives!

OUT THERE

Skydiving is always developing, as people come up with amazing new ways to skydive. From falling in unusual positions to using props, the sky is the limit for these creative skydivers!

FREEFLYING

While most skydivers freefall as if lying on their belly, brave freeflying skydivers freefall face-down or feet-down. Holding a vertical position makes skydivers fall much faster; the fastest freefliers have reached speeds of 330 miles per hour (530 km/h)!

SKYSURFING

You don't need the ocean to go surfing – to skysurf, skydivers take boards into the sky and surf across the air waves. Experienced skysurfers can do loops, rolls, and spins. The boards have special attachments to keep them attached to the skydiver's feet.

WINGSUIT FLYING

Wingsuits are made by adding extra cloth between the arms, body, and legs of a jumpsuit. This allows skydivers to glide through the air like a bird. It also slows **descent**, increasing the time the skydiver has to enjoy freefall.

DID YOU KNOW?

Like any extreme sport, skydiving is high-risk. But it's estimated that only 1 in 4,000 jumps end in injury, and 1 in 168,000 result in death. In most cases, these accidents are not due to bad equipment, but due to human error and daredevil stunts going wrong.

SKY HIGH

Skydivers are always pushing the boundaries of what's possible in this extreme sport. Since the sport began, people have been chasing the dream of jumping higher, faster, and longer, and even from the edge of space.

Joe Kittinger making history in 1960

JOE KITTINGER

Still one of the most impressive skydives of all time, Joe's skydive from 102,800 feet (31 km) in 1960 broke countless records, including highest parachute jump and fastest speed – records that he held onto for 52 years!

FELIX BAUMGARTNER

Getting closer to outer space, in 2012, Felix jumped from 25,000 feet (7.6 km) higher than Joe. On this record-breaking jump, Felix set a new type of record too – he became the first person to ever break the **sound barrier** in freefall.

ALAN EUSTACE

Maybe the most extreme skydiving record ever is held by Alan Eustace. In 2014, Alan skydived from a height of almost 136,000 feet (41.4 km) over New Mexico, USA! To get high enough, Alan was attached to a giant **helium** balloon!

DID YOU KNOW?

The higher you go, the more dangerous the conditions are. Skydivers jumping from heights over 15,000 feet (4.5 km) need to wear thick spacesuits to stay a safe temperature, and helmets that can provide enough **oxygen** to breathe.

DARING BASE JUMPING

BASE jumping is even more dangerous than regular skydiving! In this extreme sport, jumpers leap from fixed places like high buildings, cliffs, and bridges instead of moving aircraft.

SPOT THE DIFFERENCE

Similar to skydivers, BASE jumpers wear a parachute on their backs, but they only have a few seconds to open it. Unlike skydivers, most BASE jumpers don't carry a reserve parachute for when things go wrong, as there isn't time to open it!

HOW HIGH?

Because aircraft aren't used, BASE jumping is done from much lower heights than skydiving. Jumpers usually launch from between 100 and 300 metres (300 and 1,000 ft) up, which is very different from skydivers who launch thousands of metres (thousands of feet) high. But it's not without extra risks.

KNOWING THE RULES

BASE jumping has been banned in many places because of how dangerous it is. There's less official training for BASE jumpers, less safety equipment, and the locations are even riskier. The accident rate is much higher than it is for skydiving.

DID YOU KNOW?

BASE stands for all the places that these sportspeople jump from: Buildings, Antenna (such as a mast), Span (such as a bridge), and Earth (natural formations, such as a cliff).

WORLD-CLASS SKYDIVING

Being the best at skydiving isn't always about setting weird and wonderful records. Oftentimes, it's about competing against other professionals to see who will come out on top.

THINK BIG

Lots of countries hold their own national competitions, but many skydivers' sights are set on global competitions. The biggest skydiving events include the World Parachuting Championships and the FAI World Skydiving Championships, and athletes from all over the world travel to compete against each other!

TAKING THE PRIZE

Championships have lots of different events, and athletes enter events based on their best skydiving skill, whether that be speed skydiving, freestyle skydiving, team formation, or something else. Winners are usually awarded medals or trophies, and respect of course!

PLAYING FAIR

All official international skydiving championships are watched over by the International Skydiving Commission, which is a part of the FAI – the Fédération Aéronautique Internationale. This company sets rules so that events are safe and fair.

TRUE STORY

The first official World Parachuting Championships were held in 1951. It was a very small competition compared to the competitions that happen nowadays!

RECORD BREAKERS

The history books of skydiving are filled with amazing record breakers. Here are just a few of the brave people who have done impressive things and changed the way people think about skydiving.

OLDEST TANDEM SKYDIVER

The oldest person to tandem skydive is an American man called Alfred Blaschke who skydived when he was 106 years and 327 days old!

MOST SKYDIVES EVER

The world record for the most skydives in a lifetime goes to Don Kellner, who completed just over 46,000 jumps!

MOST SKYDIVES IN A DAY

Jay Stokes made a record-breaking 640 jumps within a 24-hour period in 2006!

OLDEST SOLO FEMALE SKYDIVER

In 2022, Maria Yegella, who was 84 years and 358 days old, became the oldest solo female skydiver when she jumped without being accompanied by an instructor!

WHAT IT TAKES TO BE THE BEST

It takes lots of mental and physical strength, training time, and dedication to break a world record in skydiving. Depending on the type of record, people don't always break it on their first attempt. Once the record is broken, they also have to hold onto it! This means defending your record if someone else breaks it.

GLOSSARY

Aircraft – any vehicle that travels through air. For example, planes are types of aircraft.

Altitude – the distance of an object above a surface, usually measured in comparison with sea level.

Canopy (parachute) – the fabric part of a parachute.

Descent – the journey from high in the air to the ground.

Helium – an invisible gas. Helium is lighter than air, so it's often put into balloons that are used to lift things up.

Oxygen – an invisible gas in the air that plants produce, and people and animals need to breathe.

Reserve parachute – a second, or back-up, parachute worn in case the first (main) parachute does not open properly.

Rig – another name for the backpack that skydivers wear. This holds the parachutes, AAD, and the harness system.

Sound barrier – the speed at which sound travels. When something travels faster than sound, it is said to have broken the sound barrier.

INDEX

B
BASE jumping 24-25
Baumgartner, Felix 23
Berry, Albert 9
Blaschke, Alfred 28

D
Display teams 19

E
Equipment 8-9, 21, 25
Eustace, Alan 23

F
Fédération Aéronautique Internationale (FAI) 26-27
Formations 5, 18-19, 27
Freefall 4-5, 10, 14, 18, 20-21, 23
Freeflying 20

G
Gear 6-7, 8
GPS 9

I
Instructor 10-11, 12-13, 28
International Skydiving Commission 27

K
Kellner, Don 28
Kittinger, Joe 22-23

M
McClelland, Sharon 15

P
Parachutes
Main 6, 9, 10
Reserve 6, 9, 24, 30

S
Skysurfing 21
Solo 5, 11, 12, 14-15, 28
Speed 4, 20, 23
Static line jump 5, 12-13
Stokes, Jay 28
Student 10-11, 12-13, 14

T
Tandem 5, 10-11, 28
Training 8, 13, 14, 25, 29
True stories 9, 15, 19, 22-23, 27, 28

W
Wingsuit 5, 21
World championships 17, 26-27
World records 19, 23, 26-27, 28

Y
Yegella, Maria 28

31

Copyright © 2025 Hungry Tomato Ltd

First published in 2025 by Hungry Tomato Ltd
F15, Old Bakery Studios, Blewetts Wharf,
Malpas Road, Truro, Cornwall,
TR1 1QH, UK.

No part of this publication may be reproduced, stored in a retrieval system, or transmitted in any form or by any means, electronic, mechanical, photocopying, recording, or otherwise, without prior written permission of the copyright owner.

A CIP catalogue record for this book is available from the British Library.

ISBN 9781835694275

Printed in China

Discover more at
www.hungrytomato.com

Picture Credits
(abbreviations: t = top; b = bottom; m = middle; l = left; r = right; bg = background)

Wikipedia: United States Navy with the ID 040323-N-89210-004 5bm; U.S. Air Force/Volkmar Wentzel (http://www.nationalmuseum.af.mil/Upcoming/Photos.aspx?igphoto=2000572287) 22bg; U.S. Air Force (http://www.nationalmuseum.af.mil/Upcoming/Photos.aspx?igphoto=2000572288) 23tl; Rico Shen 23bl; Shutterstock: 19tr; 21tr; Alexander_Magnum 1br; Dan_Manila 8bg; Igor Link 29m; Jackson Stock Photography 4br, 11bg; Jarun Tedjaem 32t; Jeff Schultes 17mr; JJW Photography 19ml; Joggie Botma 5tl; Mauricio Graiki FC, 2-3bg, 5tr, 5bl, 18b; Mehdi Photos 28m; Muslianshah Masrie 24-25bg; Nina Bondarchuk 17br; Pedal to the Stock 13b; Scatto61 9b; Sinesp 5br, 21ml; Scherbinator 16-17bg; Sky Antonio 5tm, 10m, 14mr, 20b; Tinseltown 23mr; ViktorKozlov 6-7bg, 14-15bg, 30-31bg; Vladimir Zhoga 26-27bg.

Every effort has been made to trace the copyright holders and we apologise in advance for any unintentional omissions. We would be pleased to insert the appropriate credit in any subsequent edition of this publication.